D0839711

WITHDRAWN

George and Martha
Washington

Portraits from the Presidential Years

∾

Ellen G. Miles

with a preface by Edmund S. Morgan

Smithsonian Institution, National Portrait Gallery

Washington, D.C.

In association with the University Press of Virginia

Charlottesville and London

An exhibition at the National Portrait Gallery,
Smithsonian Institution, Washington, D.C.
February 19–August 8, 1999

©1999 by Smithsonian Institution. All rights reserved.

Library of Congress Cataloging-in-Publication Data
Miles, Ellen Gross, 1941–
    George and Martha Washington : portraits from the presidential years / Ellen G. Miles :
with a foreword by Edmund S. Morgan.
        p.   cm.
    "An exhibition at the National Portrait Gallery, Smithsonian Institution, Washington, D.C.,
February 19–August 8, 1999"–T.p. verso.
    Includes bibliographical references.
    ISBN 0-8139-1886-3 (pbk. : alk. paper)
    1. Washington, George, 1732-1799–Portraits–Exhibitions. 2. Washington, Martha,
1731-1802–Portraits–Exhibitions. 3. Portrait painting–18th century–Exhibitions. I. National
Portrait Gallery (Smithsonian Institution) II. Title.
N7628.W3M46 1999
704.9'42'074753–dc21

                                                                                                    98-47395
Manufactured in Canada   CIP

Cover: Martha and George Washington (details; Athenaeum portraits) by Gilbert Stuart, oil on canvas, 1796. National Portrait Gallery, Smithsonian Institution, Washington, D.C.; owned jointly with the Museum of Fine Arts, Boston. Illustrated in full on pages 40 and 41.

Frontispiece: The Washington Family (detail) by Edward Savage, oil on canvas, 1789-1796. National Gallery of Art, Washington, D.C.; Andrew W. Mellon Collection, 1940.1.2. Illustrated in full on page 48.

Back cover: George Washington by John Ramage, watercolor on ivory, 1789. Mr. and Mrs. E. G. Nicholson

Photography Credits
Joseph Klima Jr.: page 8
Arthur W. Pierson, Pierson Photograph, Falls Church, Virginia: page 31
Rolland White: cover, pages 39, 40, 41, 45, 49 (George Washington)
© 1998 Board of Trustees, National Gallery of Art, Washington, D.C.: pages 2, 7, and 48
© The New-York Historical Society, New York City: page 37
© 1983 The Metropolitan Museum of Art: page 36
© 1998 The Metropolitan Museum of Art: page 23

Contents ❧

Acknowledgments / 6

Lenders to the Exhibition / 9

Preface by Edmund S. Morgan / 10

George and Martha Washington:
Portraits from the Presidential Years / 15

Notes on Sources / 52

For Further Reading / 56

Acknowledgments ∾

I would like to extend particular thanks to the lenders to this exhibition, whose interest in sharing these very special portraits of the Washingtons, and their curiosity to see them together, makes this opportunity possible. For invaluable assistance in the research for this essay, I would like to thank Sarah Keller of the University of Chicago and Sophie Cantell of Smith College for their indefatigable enthusiasm as interns on this project in the summer and fall of 1997. Museum colleagues John Wilson, Cincinnati Art Museum; Barbara Luck and Graham Hood, Colonial Williamsburg, Inc.; Edgar Munhall, the Frick Collection; Sandra Grindlay, Harvard University Art Museums; Anne Bentley, Massachusetts Historical Society; Carrie Rebora Barratt and Johanna Hecht, Metropolitan Museum of Art; Harry R. Rubenstein, National Museum of American History; Darrell Sewell, Philadelphia Museum of Art; Judy Fox, Davis Museum and Cultural Center, Wellesley College; E. McSherry Fowble, the Henry Francis DuPont Winterthur Museum; and Robin Jaffee Frank, Yale University Art Gallery, were especially helpful in the selection or research of loans. Barbara McMillan, librarian of the Mount Vernon Ladies' Association, and Dorothy Twohig and Mark Mastromarino of the George Washington Papers project, University of Virginia, were very generous with their time in answering questions about the sitters. Several colleagues at museums in the Washington area, including Stephen Patrick of the City of Bowie, Maryland, Museums; Linda Crocker Simmons of the Corcoran Gallery of Art; and Ellen McCallister Clark and Lisa Mason of the Society of the Cincinnati, Anderson House, helped with research of specific paintings. Other valuable contributions were made by Smithsonian fellow Konstantin Dierks and by Frank R. Dunaway Jr. of the Alexandria-Washington Masonic Lodge. Finally, this is a chance to thank the entire staff of the National Portrait Gallery for their myriad contributions to this and other projects. As always, special thanks go to colleagues at the Gallery whose own interests dovetailed with mine in important ways, including Robert Gordon Stewart, Margaret Christman, and Brandon Brame Fortune of the Department of Painting and Sculpture; Claire Kelly and Liza Karvellas of the Office of Exhibitions; and Linda Thrift and the staff of the Catalog of American Portraits. Especially I thank Alan Fern and Carolyn Carr for supporting staff research in American portraiture, and Frances Stevenson and Dru Dowdy, with the able assistance of Heather Egan, for making it all look so good in print.

Right
The Washington Family (detail) by Edward Savage, oil on canvas, 1789-1796. National Gallery of Art, Washington, D.C.; Andrew W. Mellon Collection, 1940.1.2. Illustrated in full on page 48.

Lenders to the Exhibition ◡

Alexandria-Washington Lodge No. 22, Ancient, Free, and Accepted Masons, Alexandria, Virginia

Cincinnati Art Museum, Ohio

The Colonial Williamsburg Foundation, Virginia

President and Fellows of Harvard College, Cambridge, Massachusetts

Historical Society of Pennsylvania, Philadelphia

Independence National Historical Park, Philadelphia

Massachusetts Historical Society, Boston

The Metropolitan Museum of Art, New York City

Mount Vernon Ladies' Association, Mount Vernon, Virginia

National Gallery of Art, Washington, D.C.

National Museum of American History, Smithsonian Institution, Washington, D.C.

National Portrait Gallery, Smithsonian Institution, Washington, D.C.

New-York Historical Society, New York City

Mr. and Mrs. E. G. Nicholson

Philadelphia Museum of Art, Pennsylvania

Wadsworth Athenaeum, Hartford, Connecticut

Yale University Art Gallery, New Haven, Connecticut

Preface ➶

Edmund S. Morgan
New Haven, Connecticut

When George Washington accepted office as President of the United States, he knew he was risking the honor and reputation he had earned by leading the country to independence and then stepping resolutely back into civilian life. He had angrily rebuffed those who suggested that he use his immense prestige to take charge of the country dictatorially. Now, less than a decade later, he was taking charge. To be sure, he was not seizing power. The people were thrusting it upon him under their new national Constitution. But they were counting on his personal honor and prestige to sustain their untried experiment in national government. If the new government succeeded, it would be his success. If it failed, for whatever reason, his honor and reputation would go down with it.

The new Constitution assigned sufficient powers to the new government to make it a success. But the old Articles of Confederation had assigned almost as large powers to the Continental Congress. The Congress had simply failed to use them, crippled by interstate rivalries and by the neglect and defiance of the separate state governments. During the 1780s, Washington had watched in dismay as the nation he had done so much to create disintegrated into thirteen little republics, fulfilling the prophecies of European pundits who had warned that large republics could never succeed. After leading an army to victory over Great Britain, Washington now had to lead a crumbling nation to victory over its own internal conflicts. What was at stake was not only his own prestige but the viability of republican government in a world of monarchies.

The weak point of republics, in contemporary opinion, was that they could not exercise power: their governments were slaves to the whims of the people they tried to govern. Power, however, was something that Washington understood. When the Continental Congress bowed low before the separate states, failing to use the powers assigned it, Washington had ruefully observed that powers left unused would sooner or later destroy their possessors, as the Continental Congress had now been destroyed. He was not about to make the same mistake. The limits imposed on him by the Constitution he never questioned, as he had never questioned his subordination to the Congress that appointed him. But within the limits set, he always took command. As President he would exercise without hesitation all the powers granted him, and he would do his best to see to it that the other branches of the national government did the same.

Right
George Washington by Rembrandt Peale, oil on canvas, 38.7 x 28.9 cm (15¼ x 11⅜ in.), 1795. The Historical Society of Pennsylvania, Philadelphia

In exercising command, Washington had never underestimated the importance of looking the part. He wanted his soldiers to look like soldiers and his officers to look like officers, standing tall, keeping their distance from the men they must lead. And the commander-in-chief must keep his distance from all of them. Power, for Washington, was necessarily a lonely business, isolating anyone who must use it from those who must be subject to it. And that isolation must be visible. To be powerful, it was essential to look powerful.

When Washington took office, no one quite knew what a President was supposed to look like. But in order to exercise the powers assigned to him, Washington recognized that he must be seen to take command, that he must endow the office with his own detached dignity. He must not look or act like a king–Americans were through with kings. Accordingly, he took pains to forbid any fancy titles. He is probably responsible for the fact that the President is still introduced in any public function simply as "the President of the United States." But he was determined that the mere title carry by itself the implication of the highest honor and respect. Under the old Continental Congress the presiding officer, also known as the President of the United States, had held open house, thereby, in Washington's view, disarming his office of whatever power it might have had. Washington would not be at home to every Tom, Dick, and Harry. Instead he held periodic levees, at which he and Martha Washington would make an appearance only to greet condescendingly the invited guests before retiring to the seclusion appropriate to the powerful. Since he was a superb horseman, he could carry the look of power in the way he rode his fine white horse (with a leopard skin saddlecloth edged in gold), or he could carry it in his elegant coach, drawn by six matched horses. Either way he could keep his distance.

Washington knew that these gestures smacked of personal ostentation, something he abhorred as dishonorable–he had turned away the authors who clamored to write his biography or publish his letters precisely because his involvement would appear ostentatious. But as President, he identified his honor wholly with the honor and power of the United States as a nation. And national honor, republican honor, required that he stand clearly above all the diverse and conflicting interests that had come together in the new government. He must neither be seen to take sides in the many disputes that occupied the new national legislature, nor must he recognize any party or faction that opposed the legal outcome of these disputes. He was the embodiment of the entire American people, empowered to see that their will be enforced against any individual, party, state, or region that opposed it.

When farmers in western Pennsylvania resisted a nationally enacted tax, he did not hesitate to march thirteen thousand militiamen to the scene, where recalcitrance dissolved before the awesome presidential presence.

Washington's conspicuous exercise of the power of his office was aimed not simply at suppressing internal conflicts among his countrymen but also at showing a united strength to the world at large, at restoring an *"American* character" that had been lost in the squabbling of the 1780s. During his presidency European powers were engaged in a life-and-death struggle for dominance. Washington was happy that the United States might become a refuge for those who suffered from the struggle, but his guiding principle was to keep his country aloof from the struggle itself, even as he kept himself above conflicts at home. One of his first acts as President was a proclamation of neutrality, and he held to that position in all his dealings with other powers. National neutrality abroad and presidential neutrality at home were the twin principles for establishing American power against the perils that confronted it. He summarized his whole policy as President in a letter to Patrick Henry toward the close of his administration in 1795: "I want an *American* character, that the powers of Europe may be convinced we act for *ourselves* and not for others; this in my judgement, is the only way to be respected abroad and happy at home." To become the partisans of Great Britain or France, he argued, would "create divisions, disturb the public tranquility, and destroy, perhaps for ever the cement which binds the Union."

Washington may have overplayed his aloofness both at home and abroad. He still keeps his distance as a national hero, with whom we can never feel familiar. But he succeeded in clothing the new government with his own honor and left the presidency with a heritage of independence and respect which, despite the antics of so many of his successors, has never quite left it.

14

George and Martha
Washington

Portraits from the Presidential Years

It is indeed almost as difficult to draw his character, as the portrait of virtue.
–Fisher Ames

In the late eighteenth century, portraits played a significant role in recalling a person's character as well as appearance, because it was believed that a person's face revealed his or her mental and emotional characteristics. This was especially true for George Washington. A study of his portraits enables us to see him from the perspective of his contemporaries, who regarded him as a man of proven virtues and leadership qualities. To understand their viewpoint, it is important to look at the portraits in the context of contemporary documents, which have often been neglected as perhaps long-winded or imprecise hyperbole.

The portraits of Washington and his wife Martha Custis that were made during Washington's years as first President of the United States depict them in images that range in size from miniatures to life-size, full-length paintings. Washington's portraits reflect the purposes for which they were made: full-length portraits commissioned by political supporters; waist-length and head-and-shoulder images made to fulfill public demand and artists' ambitions; and miniatures given to family and friends as mementos. While most of the portraits depict single figures, the largest painting is a family group that includes George (1732-1799) and Martha Washington (1731-1802), as well as Eleanor ("Nelly") Parke Custis (1779-1852) and George Washington Parke Custis (1781-1857), the children of Martha Washington's son John Parke Custis, who were adopted by the Washingtons after their father's death. Seeing the Washingtons through the eyes of the painters and the one sculptor who recorded them at life sittings, we can gain a glimpse of the Washingtons as individuals rather than as historical icons. At the same time, however, it is sometimes difficult to reconcile their divergent appearances at the hands of artists whose talent and training varied widely.

Left
George Washington by Giuseppe Ceracchi, marble, 73.3 cm (28⅞ in.) high, 1791-1795. Signed: "Ceracchi faciebat Philadelphia 1795". The Metropolitan Museum of Art, New York City; bequest of John L. Cadwalader, 1914

Contemporary Descriptions

Several contemporary descriptions of the Washingtons help us to see them as they were seen during their lifetime. An English visitor to Mount Vernon in 1785 described Washington:

> The General is about six feet high, perfectly straight and well made; rather inclined to be lusty. His eyes are full and blue and seem to express an air of gravity. His nose inclines to the aquiline; his mouth small; his teeth are yet good and his cheeks indicate perfect health. His forehead is a noble one and he wears his hair turned back, without curls and quite in the officer's style, and tyed in a long queue behind. Altogether he makes a most noble, respectable appearance.

Senator William Maclay of Pennsylvania wrote on January 20, 1791, on the occasion of a dinner with the President:

> Let me take a review of him As he really is. In stature about Six feet, with An Unexceptionable Make, but lax Appearance, his frame Would seem to Want filling Up. his Motions rather slow than lively, tho he showed no Signs of having suffered either by Gout or Rheumatism. his complexion pale Nay Almost Cadaverous. his Voice hollow and indistinct Owing As I believe to Artificial teeth before in his Upper Jaw.

And Isaac Weld Jr., an Englishman who visited the United States in 1795-1797, published a description of Washington:

> The height of his person is about five feet eleven; his chest is full; and his limbs, though rather slender, well shaped and muscular. His head is small, in which respect he resembles the make of a great number of his countrymen. His eyes are of a light grey colour; and, in proportion to the length of his face, his nose is long. Mr. Stewart, the eminent portrait painter, told me, there are features in his face totally different from what he ever observed in that of any other human being; the sockets of the eyes, for instance, are larger than what he ever met with before, and the upper part of the nose broader. All his features, he observed, were indicative of the strongest and most ungovernable passions, and had he been born in the forests, it was his opinion that he would have been the fiercest man amongst the savage tribes.

Martha Washington's manner and appearance were described by Abigail Adams in 1789 in letters to her sister Mary Cranch. After her first meeting with Mrs. Washington in New York, she wrote: "She received me with great ease & politeness. She is plain in her dress, but that plainness is the best of every article. . . . Her Hair is white, her Teeth beautifull, her person rather short than otherways. . . . Her manners are modest and unassuming, dignified and femenine, not the Tincture of ha'ture about her." Two weeks later she commented: "Mrs. Washington is one of those unassuming characters which create Love & Esteem. A most becoming pleasentness sits upon her countanance & an unaffected deportment which renders her the object of veneration and Respect." After a family outing with the Washingtons, she added: "Mrs. Washington is a most friendly, good Lady, always pleasent and easy, doatingly fond of her Grandchildren, to whom she is quite the Grandmamma." In June 1794, when Henry Wansey, an Englishman in the wool trade, visited Philadelphia, he described Martha as appearing "something older than the President, though I understand, they were both born in the same year; short in stature, rather robust; very plain in her dress, wearing a very plain cap, with her grey hair closely turned up under it."

George Washington by Jean-Antoine Houdon, plaster life mask, 31.8 cm (12½ in.) high, 1785. Pierpont Morgan Library, New York [not in exhibition]

Portrait Miniatures

By the time of his election to the presidency in 1789, George Washington had been portrayed from life by six artists, including Charles Willson Peale (1741-1827), who painted the first portrait of Washington in 1772, and French sculptor Jean-Antoine Houdon (1741-1828), whose life mask, made in 1785, is the most accurate representation that we have of Washington's face. By the time of his election, Washington was very familiar with the experience of sitting for a portrait, writing in 1785 about his portrait sitting for English portrait painter Robert Edge Pine (1720s-1788):

> In for a penny, in for a pound is an old adage. I am so hackneyed to the touches of the Painters pencil, that I am now altogether at their beck, and sit like patience on a Monument, whilst they are delineating the lines of my face.
>
> It is a proof among many others, of what habit & custom can effect. At first I was as impatient at the request, and as restive under the operation, as a Colt is of the Saddle– The next time, I submitted very reluctantly, but with less flouncing. Now, no dray moves more readily to the Thill, than I do to the Painters Chair.

As President, he was frequently asked to give time for sittings, with the result that he sat for more than a dozen artists over the next eight years. He came to find the process time-consuming, and the artists' plans to

George Washington by
John Ramage, watercolor
on ivory, 5.4 x 3.8 cm (2⅛ x
1½ in.), 1789. Mr. and Mrs.
E. G. Nicholson

duplicate and sell their portraits very bothersome. And although Martha Washington was not as frequently portrayed as her husband, she had a role in the commission of some of his portraits, and was the recipient of the gift of portraits from artists who hoped for recognition or political favors in return.

In the presidential portraits, Washington is most often depicted wearing a black velvet suit with a white shirt trimmed with a plain ruffle. His hair is powdered and tied in a queue with a black silk bow or ribbon. Some artists depicted the residue of white powder that fell onto his shoulders. Henrietta Liston, wife of British ambassador Robert Liston, described Washington in such a black velvet suit at his last address to Congress in December 1796. She noted that "about twelve oClock Washington entered in full dress, as He always is on publick occasions, black velvet, sword &c." In five portraits, however, Washington is instead depicted in a blue and buff uniform that resembles the one worn by general officers of the United States Army. In two of these portraits he wears the badge of the Society of the Cincinnati, the honorific organization founded by his officers after the war. Both the black velvet suit and the uniform are therefore intentional aspects of the portraits. Edward Savage and John Trumbull each portrayed Washington both ways. Savage, for example, in 1789 completed one portrait of him in uniform and apparently began another portrait, which he later described as "the portrait I first Sketched in black Velvet" (Art Institute of Chicago).

The first two portraits made during Washington's presidency were miniatures. Both were painted on October 3, 1789, in New York City, the first temporary capital of the United States. These images, painted on ivory, were meant for personal use by family or close friends. The first was painted for Martha Washington by Irish miniaturist John Ramage (circa 1748-1802). The President noted the sittings in his diary [illustrated on page 8]: "Sat for Mr. Rammage near two hours to day, who was drawing a miniature Picture of me for Mrs. Washington." Washington is shown in his uniform, wearing the badge of the Society of the Cincinnati. The miniature's case encloses a lock of his hair and is decorated with his initials. Ramage, trained at the Dublin Society Schools, came to New York in 1777, when the city was occupied by the British army. He worked there as a miniaturist until 1794. The details of the commission are not known. Ramage made a second version of this portrait for himself, showing Washington facing the viewer (Robert Hull Fleming Museum, University of Vermont), and also made duplicates of each miniature.

On the same day that Washington sat for Ramage, he posed for the Marquise de Bréhan (born 1752?), who was the sister-in-law of Eléanor-François-Elie, Comte de Moustier, minister to the United States from the court of France. Washington noted: "Sat about two Oclock for Madam de

Brehan to complete a Miniature profile of me which she had begun from
Memory and which she had made exceedingly like the Original." (Washington used the word "original" to refer to himself, as the model for the
portrait.) The cameolike portrait is in the neoclassical style, in the form
of a sculpted relief, and represents Washington wearing a laurel wreath, a
symbol of victory. A similar cameolike miniature of Nelly Custis is
framed on the reverse. Madame de Bréhan, a talented amateur artist,
may have begun Washington's portrait when she and her brother-in-law
first met him at Mount Vernon a year earlier, in November 1788. Or she
may have copied a sculpture, perhaps the one by Jean-Antoine Houdon
or by Joseph Wright. The sitting on October 3 took place just before their
return to Paris, where Moustier arranged to have the portrait engraved.
He sent several prints to Washington in 1790:

> Accept, with goodness, I pray, Sir, the homage which I have the honor to
> make in the accompanying proofs–Mad. de Brehan will profit of the first
> certain opportunity which presents to address to Madam Washington the
> medallion intended for her–in the mean time, She will make a copy of the
> original for herself.

Washington later gave a watercolor version of this portrait to Anne
Willing Bingham, wife of wealthy Philadelphia merchant William
Bingham, and gave engravings to Mary Morris, the wife of Senator
Robert Morris, and Deborah Stewart, the wife of General Walter Stewart.
To Mrs. Bingham he wrote: "In presenting the enclosed (with compli-

ments to Mrs Bingham) the President fulfils a promise. Not for the representation;–not for the value;–but as the production of a fair hand, the offering is made, and the acceptan[ce] of it requested."

State Portraits

Unlike these miniatures, most portraits painted during the presidential years were of a public nature. Many resulted from specific requests from admiring individuals and groups. The first two requests came during Washington's trip to New England in the fall of 1789. In Boston, the city selectmen asked for a portrait for Faneuil Hall

> in behalf of the Ladies, who are ambitious of transmitting to their Children a perfect likeness of their justly Beloved President at the moment he blessed them with his presence; when his benign countenance made such an impression on their hearts as they wish to recognize in his Portrait, in future.

Washington, with a busy schedule, declined to sit, but offered "that I would have it drawn when I returned to New York, if there was a good Painter there–or by Mr. Trumbull when he should arrive; and would send it to them." However, Christian Gullager (1759-1826), a Danish artist who had settled in Massachusetts, took advantage of the opportunity. According to Salem clergyman Dr. Jeremy Belknap, while Washington was at a concert in King's Chapel, "Gullager, the painter stole a likeness of him from a Pew behind the pulpit. N.B. Gullager followed Gen W. to Portsm where he sat 2½ hours for him to take his portrait wh he did & obtained a very good likeness" [illustrated overleaf]. Washington recorded the sitting in his diary on November 3: "Sat two hours in the forenoon for a Mr. [ ] Painter of Boston, at the Request of Mr. Brick of that place; who wrote Majr. Jackson that it was an earnest desire of many of the Inhabitants of that Town that he might be endulged." According to the artist's son Charles Gulager in 1832, "at the time the likeness of Washington was taken the citizens of Boston offered him Five Hundred dollars for it that it might be placed in Faneuil Hall but it was refused." Instead, Belknap acquired the portrait after a raffle.

The second New England portrait [illustrated overleaf] was the result of Washington's visit to Harvard College on October 29, 1789, when Joseph Willard, president of the college, showed him the scientific instruments in the Philosophical Hall ("philosophy" was the term then used to describe the physical sciences). Willard wrote Washington on November 7:

George Washington by
Christian Gullager, oil on
canvas, 76.8 x 67.3 cm (30¼
x 26½ in.), 1789.
Massachusetts Historical
Society, Boston

Right
George Washington by
Edward Savage, oil on
canvas, 76.2 x 63.5 cm (30 x
25 in.), 1789/1790. Signed:
"E. Savage Pinx 1790".
Harvard University Portrait
Collection, Cambridge,
Massachusetts; gift of
Edward Savage to Harvard
College, 1791

Far right
*George Washington before
the Battle of Trenton* by
John Trumbull, oil on
canvas, 67.3 x 47 cm (26½ x
18½ in.), circa 1792. The
Metropolitan Museum of
Art, New York City; bequest
of Grace Wilkes, 1922

When you were in the Philosophy Chamber of the University in this place, you may perhaps remember, that I expressed my wishes, that your Portrait might, some time or other, adorn that Room. Since that, Mr Savage, the Bearer of this, who is a Painter, and is going to New York, has called on me, and of his own accord, has politely and generously offered to take your Portrait for the University, if you will be so kind as to sit. As it would be exceedingly grateful to all the Governors of this literary Society that the Portrait of the Man we so highly love, esteem and revere, should be the property of, and be placed within Harvard College, permit me, Sir, to request the favor of your sitting for the purpose.

Edward Savage, an ambitious, self-taught Massachusetts painter and engraver, delivered Willard's letter after Washington returned to New York. Washington agreed to sit "from a wish that I have to gratify . . . every reasonable desire of the patrons & promoters of Science–And at the same time I feel myself flattered by the polite manner in which I am requested to give this proof of my sincere regard & good wishes for the prosperity of the University of Cambridge." He sat for about seven hours, in three sittings. The painting shows Washington in his army uniform with the badge of the Society of the Cincinnati on the lapel. Washington sat again on April 6 so that Savage could paint a replica for John Adams (Adams National Historic Site).

John Trumbull (1756–1843) painted two state portraits of Washington in 1790 and 1791. Between 1790 and 1793, Trumbull had numerous sittings with Washington–twelve in 1790 alone. His state portraits and history paintings primarily depict Washington in his military role during the Revolution, which is appropriate. Trumbull, a painter from Connecticut, served in the American army for more than a year during the war, briefly in 1775 as Washington's aide-de-camp. His training as an artist in England in the 1780s led him to prefer history painting, a form of contemporary art that emphasized accurate renderings of recent national events, especially the heroic acts of leaders. In the summer of 1790, Trumbull painted his first life-size full-length portrait of Washington for New York City Hall (where it remains today), prior to the move of the national capital from New York to Philadelphia. In May 1791, during Washington's visit to South Carolina, the city council of Charleston commissioned a second life-size full-length portrait (Yale University Art Gallery) "to commemorate his arrival in the metropolis of this State, and to hand down to posterity the remembrance of the man to whom they are so much indebted for the blessings of peace, liberty and independence." Trumbull's small painting of Washington [illustrated on page 23] repeats the composition of the large portrait. Trumbull later described the Charleston full-length as "the best certainly of those which I painted." He chose to give his military character, in the most sublime moment of its exertion–the evening previous to the Battle of Princeton. . . . I told the President my object; he entered into it warmly, and, as the work advanced, we talked of the scene, its dangers, its almost desperation. He looked the scene again, and I happily transferred to the canvass, the lofty expression of his animated countenance, the high resolve to conquer or to perish.

South Carolina Congressman William Loughton Smith, while "personally pleased . . . thought the city would be better satisfied with a more matter-of-fact likeness, such as they had recently seen him–calm, tranquil, peaceful." Trumbull reluctantly asked the President for additional sittings:

> Oppressed as the President was with business, I was reluctant to ask him to sit again. I however waited upon him, stated Mr. Smith's objection, and he cheerfully submitted to a second penance, adding, "Keep this picture for yourself, Mr. Trumbull, and finish it to your own taste."

Martha Washington by Edward Savage, oil on canvas, 76.2 x 63.5 cm (30 x 25 in.), 1790. U.S. Department of the Interior, National Park Service, Adams National Historic Site, Quincy, Massachusetts [not in exhibition]

This second portrait was unveiled in Charleston in July 1792.

Another portrait request in 1790 came from the Tammany Society in New York City. However, this request was not successful. Washington's secretary, Tobias Lear, wrote on August 24 to John Marsden Pintard that he was directed by the President

> to inform you that it is with regret he must decline the honor which the St. Tammany's society would do him by having his Portrait taken. The President is detained now in this city only by some particular business with the heads of the Executive departments, in which he is constantly engaged, and desireous of dispatching as soon as possible, being anxious to get to Virg[ini]a. He therefore requests that you will be so good as to present his best thanks to the Society for their politeness, and he trusts they will consider his declining their request in its proper light.

The two portraits of Martha Washington that were painted in 1790 and 1791 were of a more personal nature. Edward Savage (1761-1817) painted the first in 1790 for John Adams, as a pendant to the portrait that Adams had commissioned of George Washington. The second was a miniature (now unlocated) painted in 1791 by Charles Willson Peale for one of Martha's granddaughters–Martha, Nelly, or Elizabeth ("Eliza") Custis, the children of her son John Parke Custis. Payment on June 6, 1791, is the only documentation for the portrait: "pd. Mr. Peale for taking a minia-ture of Mrs. Washington for Miss Custis & retouching some other pieces for Mrs. Washington, 15 [dollars]." Peale at the time was touching up miniatures that he had painted in 1771 of John Parke Custis and his sister Martha Parke Custis, who were both deceased by 1791.

European Artists and American Admirers

In the early 1790s Washington was also portrayed by several European artists who came to the United States, attracted by the new, democratic American system of government. The first of these was Giuseppe Ceracchi (1751-1801), an Italian sculptor with a strong republican polit-ical philosophy. He hoped to win the commission for the equestrian monument to George Washington that was approved by Congress in 1783. Arriving in January 1791, he submitted a plan that fall for "A Monument Designed to Perpetuate the Memory of American Liberty," which included a bronze equestrian statue of Washington wearing a Roman toga. To encourage support for his design, he modeled terra-cotta portraits of influential political figures, including Washington, who later recalled that he agreed to pose "with the reluctance which he has always felt on these occasions." After the committee of the House of Representatives postponed the decision to commission the monument, Ceracchi returned to Europe. In Amsterdam he exhibited his terra-cotta portrait of Washington. He wrote to Martha Washington on July 16, 1792, "Besides the generality of Gentilmen, all the Ladyes in Oland are ravished at the sight of my model that rappresents General Washington, what dignity they sais, what solidity shows in his mind; happy must be the Lady that possesses his heart." Ceracchi then went to Italy, where he carved some of his American portraits in marble, including that of Washington. He shipped the bust [illustrated on page 14] from Florence to the Washingtons, eliciting an acknowledgment from Martha, who wrote on March 17, 1794, that she "finds herself at a loss for words to express her sensibility for the marble representation of the President which he sent her; and which she thinks, both in workmanship, and resemblance of the original, does great credit to the masterly hand from which it proceeded."

Scottish artist Archibald Robertson (1765-1835) also came to the United States in 1791. He painted miniatures of George and Martha Washington as the first step in a commission for Washington's portrait from the President's Scottish admirer, David Steuart Erskine, eleventh Earl of Buchan. Robertson planned to settle in New York City and agreed to bring, as a gift from Buchan for Washington, a small wooden box made

George Washington by
Archibald Robertson,
watercolor on ivory, 6.4 x
5.4 cm (2½ x 2⅛ in.),
1791-1792. The Colonial
Williamsburg Foundation,
Virginia

Martha Washington by
Archibald Robertson,
watercolor on ivory, 6.4 x
5.4 cm (2½ x 2⅛ in.),
1791-1792. The Colonial
Williamsburg Foundation,
Virginia

from the oak tree that had sheltered Sir William Wallace after the Battle of Falkirk. Referring to Washington as "the modern American Wallace," Buchan wrote that the new American "federal government" with Washington as President pleased "the host of enlightened and liberal-minded Scottish patriots of every rank, who, deploring the abuses of the government under which they were born, rejoiced in the happiness of their trans-atlantic kinsmen." He introduced Robertson as "an honest artist seeking for bread & for fame in the New World." He asked Washington "to send me your Portrait that I may place it among those whom I most honour. Whether Mr Robertson may be equal to the task I know not but I beg leave to reccomend him to yr countenance." Visiting the Washington family in Philadelphia, Robertson recorded his own uneasiness on meeting the President:

> The excitation in the mind of the stranger was evidently obvious to Washington, for from his ordinary cold and distant address he declined into the most easy and familiar intercourse in conversation. . . . Washington easily penetrated into the heart and feelings of Lord Buchan's friend, and he left no means untried to make him feel perfectly at ease in his company during the period he intended to spend with him in Philadelphia.

Mrs. Washington's "easy, polished and familiar gayety, and ceaseless cheerfulness, almost accomplished a cure, by the aid of her grandchildren, G. W. Custis and Miss Eleanor Custis." Robertson later wrote the Earl of Buchan that Washington "very readily condescended to sit for his likeness to me—but as it was utterly impracticable for me to get my apparatus for Portrait Painting conveyed to Philad[paper torn] & at the same time I was uncertain even of his sitting, I wa[s] under the necessity of making a miniature of a pretty [paper torn] size, from which I copy one for your Lordship." He completed the watercolor-on-ivory life portraits by January 11, 1792. His depiction of the President in a plum-colored coat, and Martha Washington in a red dress with a black lace shawl, are unusual in their choice of the color of the clothing. Robertson kept the miniatures "in his family as an heirloom, and memorial of his veneration for the great and successful champion of American liberty." Next he painted the oil portrait for the earl's "collection of portraits of the most celebrated worthies in liberal principles and in useful literature." Robertson struggled to complete it, and it was finally delivered in November 1793. Margaret Fraser, Lady Buchan, sent Martha Washington a portrait of the earl in return, probably a paste bas-relief by James Tassie.

John Trumbull's close association with the President also resulted in three small portraits intended for the Washingtons' personal use. In July

1790, he presented a small full-length of Washington (Henry Francis du Pont Winterthur Museum) to Martha Washington "in evidence of my profound and affectionate respect." Two small oil portraits [illustrated on page 30] were probably also gifts from the artist. The portrait of Martha is a copy of one that Trumbull had painted in 1792, while that of Washington is a reduced version of a larger portrait painted in 1793 (both Yale University Art Gallery). The portrait of Washington in his black velvet suit is one of only four by Trumbull that show the President in civilian dress. The two paintings may be the ones that were delivered to Washington on June 18, 1793, the date of a notation in Washington's household account book: "gave Mr. Trumbull's servant who bro't pictures .50 [fifty cents]." Both portraits are in their original frames, perhaps the work of Philadelphia carver and gilder James Reynolds, who was paid $3.33 about two months later "for 2 picture frames."

The demands on Washington's time for portrait sittings led him in July 1792 to turn down a request from American artist William Joseph Williams (1759-1823). Governor Henry Lee of Virginia wrote Washington to introduce the artist, saying that Williams "promised to present the portrait to the C'Wealth in case it should be a good one, by which means we shall have the gratification of beholding daily the semblance of our beloved and illustrious countryman." Washington wrote Lee on July 3, describing Williams as

> a professional man, [who] may, or may not be, a luminary of the first magnitude for aught I know to the contrary. But to be frank, and I hope you will not be displeased with me for being so, I am so heartily tired of the attendance which, from one cause or another, I have bestowed on these kind of people, that it is now more than two years since I have resolved to sit no more for any of them; and have adhered to it; except in instances where it has been requested by public bodies, or for a particular purpose (not of the Painters) and could not, without offence, be refused.

> I have been led to make this resolution for another reason besides the irksomeness of sitting, and the time I loose by it, which is, that these productions have, in my estimation, been made use of as a sort of tax upon individuals, by being engraved, and that badly, and hawked, or advertised for Sale.

Williams wrote Lee that "he will, however, sit on the application of the Executive body–This was obliged to be done for Mr. Trumbull, who has just taken the President's Likeness for the City of Charles Town." Williams offered the Alexandria (Virginia) Masonic Lodge No. 22 a portrait of Washington if the lodge would request the sittings. The lodge voted in favor of this on August 29, 1793, writing to Washington, "but although history shall hand down your virtues and patriotic services to

George Washington by
John Trumbull, oil on
mahogany panel, 9.7 x 8.3
cm (3¹³/₁₆ x 3¼ in.), circa
1793. Signed on reverse:
"J.T." National Museum of
American History,
Smithsonian Institution,
Washington, D.C.

Martha Washington by
John Trumbull, oil on
mahogany panel, 9.8 x 7.3
cm (3⅞ x 2⅞ in.), circa
1793. Signed on reverse:
"J.T." National Museum of
American History,
Smithsonian Institution,
Washington, D.C.

George Washington by
William Joseph Williams,
pastel on paper, 71.1 x 55.8
cm (28 x 22 in.), 1794.
Signed: "W. Williams
Pinxit 1794". Alexandria-
Washington Lodge No. 22,
Ancient, Free, and
Accepted Masons,
Alexandria, Virginia

the latest posterity, and although the name of *George Washington* must ever be dear to every good Mason . . . yet it be a source of the most refined gratification the tracing out and contemplating the various ornaments of his character in the resemblance of his person." The date of the sitting is given in an inscription that was once on the back of the portrait: "Williams Pinxit ad vivum in Philadelphia [Williams painted from life in Philadelphia], September 18, 1794." The lodge received the portrait [illustrated on page 31] that October. Washington is shown as a Virginia past master, in a black coat with Masonic regalia and jewels. Williams painted the most closely observed portrait of Washington as President, including a scar on his left cheek, a mole under his right ear, and smallpox scars on his nose and cheeks.

A third European artist who depicted Washington was Swedish painter Adolph-Ulrich Wertmüller (1751-1811), who came to Philadelphia in May 1794 to escape the turmoil of the French Revolution. The sittings are not documented. The portrait, perhaps painted in the Senate Chamber, was completed on November 8, according to the artist's records, where it is described as showing the first President of Congress dressed in black velvet. George Washington Parke Custis later wrote: "Of the painting . . . we literally know nothing . . . through whose influence was the sitting obtained for a picture said to be for a Swedish nobleman?" The sittings could have been arranged by Richard Söderstrom, the Swedish consul in Philadelphia, or William Loughton Smith, congressman from South Carolina, two of the artist's first sitters in the United States. American painter Rembrandt Peale later described Wertmüller's purpose in painting Washington:

> Ambitious of drawing himself into notice, he obtained the consent of Washington to sit for his portrait. It was, as usual, a highly decorated painting, but dark in the coloring and had a German aspect. It was but little admired, and soon ceased to be spoken of or noticed in his room where it hung between two open windows.

When Wertmüller's friend Carl Fredrik Sundvall saw a version of the portrait in Sweden, he praised the artist for having "the good fortune to paint the man who for eternity will be famed in world history, the illustrious Washington, America's protecting angel and the founder of a free nation. To this man, so precious to humanity, to philosophy, and to the peoples' welfare, statues should be raised in all America's cities, and portraits hung in all the courtrooms."

Giuseppe Ceracchi, the Italian sculptor who first made Washington's portrait in 1791/92, returned to the United States in 1794 after he was expelled from Rome and Tuscany because of his support of the French Revolution. He redesigned his proposal for the monument to Wash-

Right
George Washington by Adolph-Ulrich Wertmüller, oil on canvas, 64.5 x 53.7 cm (25⅜ x 21⅛ in.), 1794. Signed: "A: Wertmüller. S. P^t. Philadelphia 1794." Philadelphia Museum of Art, Pennsylvania; gift of Mr. and Mrs. John Wagner

ington, replacing his figure with one of the Goddess of Liberty. He organized a campaign to enlist subscribers, with Washington's name prominently on the list. He also asked for new sittings to modify the portrait of Washington that had been carved in marble in Florence [illustrated on page 14]. The President's secretary, Bartholomew Dandridge, wrote that Washington

> complied on the same principle which had produced the first sitting: always conceiving, that it was for purposes of your own it was wanted until hints were given that it was designed to be presented to Mrs. Washington. Then for the first time he knew and declared that he could not, and would not accept it as a present.

Soon Ceracchi, lacking support for the monument, returned Washington's subscription funds and then sent Washington a bill, asking "For the Original *marble* bust *Dollars* 1500." Washington refused to pay such a high price for a portrait he had not commissioned, and the angry Ceracchi asked for the return of the sculpture. Washington complied, expressing regret that "the abilities of our infant republic will not afford employment for a person of your talents." Ceracchi sold the bust of Washington to Josef de Jaudenes y Nebot, chargé d'affaires from the court of Spain, and left for France.

Family Portraits

Washington was more willing to satisfy requests for portraits from his family. Martha Washington's sixteen-year-old granddaughter Martha Parke Custis asked Washington for his portrait in the fall of 1794, before her marriage to Thomas Peter. The President agreed to have one painted, teasing her that he never would imagine that "the wish nearest a young girl's heart on the eve of marriage was to possess an old man's picture." Her older sister Eliza wrote Washington on September 7 that she, too, had

> no other wish nearer my heart than that of possessing your likeness. . . . It is my first wish to have it in my power to contemplate, at all times, the features of one, who, I so highly respect as the Father of his country and look up to with greatful affection as a parent to myself and family.

Washington agreed also to give her a miniature, writing a letter with tender advice about her romantic expectations of marriage. The miniatures (Tudor Place Foundation, Inc., and Mount Vernon Ladies' Association) were painted by Irish miniaturist Walter Robertson (circa 1750–1801). The artist had come to the United States in 1793 from Dublin with American portrait painter Gilbert Stuart. According to William Dunlap, a contemporary American artist, he "went to Philadelphia before Stuart, and painted a portrait, in miniature, of Washington." Robertson depicted Washington in uniform. This suggests that the sittings took place just before or after the President's expedition to western Pennsylvania to subdue the local taxpayers' revolt known as the Whiskey Rebellion. Washington left Philadelphia on September 30 and returned on October 28. His household account book lists payment on November 25, 1794: "pd Wm Robertson for painting two pictures of the President & one of Mrs. Washington 170 [dollars]." (The miniature of Martha Washington was probably destroyed during the Civil War.)

Robertson kept a version of the portrait for himself. Like the others, this miniature depicts the President in uniform, but with a black neckband instead of a white one. Dunlap wrote that the portrait "was altogether a failure; and so little like the General that one might doubt his sitting for it." He objected to the depiction in part because

George Washington by Walter Robertson, watercolor on ivory, 9.5 x 7.3 cm (3¾ x 2⅞ in.), 1794. Cincinnati Art Museum, Ohio; gift of Mr. and Mrs. Charles Fleischmann, in memory of Julius Fleischmann

> one remarkable deviation from the General's costume adds to the belief that he did not sit for it—it is painted with a black stock, an article of dress he never wore. I believe, when President, Washington never wore his military dress; when he, as General, wore it, he always wore it, but with a white cambrick stock.

In 1795 Robertson, with English miniaturist Robert Field (circa 1769–1819) and Irish engraver John James Barralet (circa 1747–1815), announced plans to publish an engraving of the portrait. It would be sold with other prints that celebrated Washington's part in subduing the Whiskey Rebellion. Field wrote to his Baltimore patron Robert Gilmore Jr. on January 13, 1795, that the

> miniature of the President is as good a likeness and as fine a piece of painting as ever I saw. I have engaged to engrave it the same size with some ornaments to surround & make it more interesting, but as Mr. R. is determined to go to India early in the summer, he has declined the large plate and offers to sell me the picture.

The artists advertised the print with "a Portrait of Alexander Hamilton, Late secretary of the Treasury . . . Also An Equestrian Portrait of the President, attended by Colonel Hamilton, as his aid-de-camp." In

George Washington (Gibbs-
Channing-Avery portrait)
by Gilbert Stuart, oil on
canvas, 76.8 x 64.1 cm
(30¼ x 25¼ in.), 1795. The
Metropolitan Museum of
Art, New York City; Rogers
Fund, 1907

George Washington by
Charles Willson Peale, oil
on canvas, 73.7 x 60.3 cm
(29 x 23¾ in.), 1795. The
New-York Historical
Society, New York City; gift
of Thomas J. Bryan, 1867

addition, "Four Plates in Commemoration of the Western Expedition" would be engraved after drawings by Barralet. However, only the plate with the image of Washington was published. Robertson probably did sell the miniature before leaving Philadelphia. Its next recorded owner was Ernst Frederik Walterstorff (1755–1820), governor of the Danish West Indies from 1787 to 1796, who visited the United States in 1796.

Portraits by Gilbert Stuart and the Peales

The best known portraits of Washington as President were made in 1795 and 1796 by Gilbert Stuart, Charles Willson Peale, and Rembrandt Peale. Stuart (1755–1828), an American artist, returned from eighteen years in Britain and Ireland in 1793. According to Irish painter John Dowling Herbert, Stuart's ambition was to paint Washington: "I expect to make a fortune by Washington." Stuart went to Philadelphia in the late autumn of 1794, with a letter of introduction from Chief Justice John Jay, expressly to paint the President. The sitting or sittings probably took place that winter or, according to Stuart's daughter Jane Stuart, "toward the spring of 1795." It is assumed that the portrait was completed by April 20, 1795, when Stuart compiled "A list of gentlemen who are to have copies of the Portrait of the President of the United States." The thirty-two names included that of Philadelphia merchant John Vaughan, who ordered two copies, sending one (National Gallery of Art) to London to his father Samuel, an English merchant who had lived in Philadelphia. This ownership gave the name "Vaughan" to the type of portrait by Stuart that shows Washington facing to the right. Engraved in London in 1796, the portrait was included in the third volume of Henry Hunter's English translation of Johann Caspar Lavater's *Essays on Physiognomy*. This publication presents Lavater's theories about the ways that one can understand a person's character and personality from the shape of the face and its individual features. Basing his analysis of Washington's physiognomy on two other engravings of Washington, Lavater commented that an oblong face, "when not too angular, always indicates phlegm and firmness." He added that "every thing in this face announces the good man, a man upright, of simple manners, sincere, firm, reflecting and generous."

Stuart painted at least a dozen replicas of this first portrait. Most of them show Washington in his black velvet suit with plain black buttons, in front of a red curtain or a red or neutral background. A few show him in a brown coat with yellow metal buttons, in front of a green curtain. The example that became the property of the Gibbs family of Rhode

Island, who were friends of the artist, has a unique combination of Washington in a black coat in front of a green curtain [illustrated on page 36]. Close study shows, however, that a layer of opaque brown paint is visible under the black coat, and X-rays reveal the use of white paint in highlights on the buttons that are now overpainted in black. Thus Washington's clothing may have been changed in this painting to a black velvet coat from a brown one, a more informal color. Such a coat was described by a contemporary, who said that at Mrs. Washington's receptions the President wore "some colored coat and waistcoat, (the only one recollected was brown, with bright buttons)." Such a change in the color of the coat supports the tradition in the Gibbs family that the portrait remained for some time in Stuart's studio and was retouched by the artist.

Charles Willson Peale and his son Rembrandt Peale (1778–1860) also painted Washington's portrait in 1795 [illustrated on pages 37 and 11]. Like John Trumbull, Charles Willson Peale had fought in the Revolutionary War at Washington's side. He became Washington's most employed portrait painter in the 1770s and 1780s, when he made more than fifty portraits of the general. The portrait sittings in 1795 occurred, it is believed, because of a commission to Rembrandt Peale from Henry William DeSaussure of South Carolina, at the time of his resignation as director of the United States Mint. The sittings took place in Philadelphia's Philosophical Hall, where the elder Peale had installed his museum in the fall of 1794. Rembrandt recorded three morning sittings, which probably took place in late October or early November:

> It was in the Autumn of 1795 that, at my father's request, Washington consented to sit to me—and the hour he appointed was seven o'clock in the morning. I was up before day-light, putting everything in the best condition for the sitting with which I was to be honored; but before the hour arrived, became so agitated that I could scarcely mix my colours, and was conscious that my anxiety would overpower me, and that I should fail in my purpose, unless my father would agree to take a Canvass alongside of me, and thus give me an assurance that the sittings would not be unprofitable, by affording a double chance for a likeness. This had the

George Washington by Thomas Holloway, after Gilbert Stuart, line engraving, 23 x 19.7 cm (9^{1}/$_{16}$ x 7¾ in.), 1796. National Portrait Gallery, Smithsonian Institution, Washington, D.C.

Martha Washington
(Athenaeum portrait) by
Gilbert Stuart, oil on
canvas, 121.9 x 94 cm (48 x
37 in.), 1796. National
Portrait Gallery,
Smithsonian Institution,
Washington, D.C.; owned
jointly with the Museum of
Fine Arts, Boston

George Washington
(Athenaeum portrait) by
Gilbert Stuart, oil on
canvas, 121.9 x 94 cm (48 x
37 in.), 1796. National
Portrait Gallery,
Smithsonian Institution,
Washington, D.C.; owned
jointly with the Museum of
Fine Arts, Boston

effect to calm my nerves, & I enjoyed the rare advantage of studying the desired Countenance whilst in familiar conversation with my father.

Viewing the results gives an extraordinary combined view of Washington. Both portraits show him in a black velvet coat with a standing collar, a coat very similar to that seen in Stuart's portrait of the same year. At the sitting, Rembrandt placed himself directly in front of Washington, with his father on his right. From the direction that Washington is facing in each portrait, it is possible to imagine him as he looked at the sitting, in the presence of the two artists.

This first sitting was attended only by Charles Willson and Rembrandt Peale. Rembrandt's uncle James Peale (1749–1831) and brother Raphaelle Peale (1774–1825) were admitted to the second and third sittings, as was his younger brother Titian (1780–1798), only fifteen years old. James sat on Rembrandt's left, making a miniature, and Raphaelle was seated further to the left, making a profile drawing. (These portraits have not survived.) This led to a famous pun. Stuart later told artist William Dunlap that it was at his request

> that General Washington, after sitting to him, consented to sit once more to Mr. Peale, and related the result somewhat in this manner to Mr. Neagle. "I looked in to see how the old gentleman was getting on with the picture, and to my astonishment, I found the general surrounded by the whole family. They were peeling him, sir. As I went away I met Mrs. Washington, 'Madam,' said I, 'the general's in a perilous situation.' 'How, sir?' 'He is beset, madam—no less than five upon him at once; one aims at his eye—another at his nose—another is busy with his hair—his mouth is attacked by a fourth—and the fifth has him by the button; in short, madam, there are five painters at him, and you who know how much he has suffered when only attended by one, can judge of the horrors of his situation.'"

Charles Willson Peale exhibited his portrait of Washington in his museum. As its pendant, he painted a portrait of Martha Washington. His familiarity with the Washingtons led him to propose this new portrait. According to Rembrandt Peale,

> His father, Charles Willson Peale, in 1795, met General Washington in the market, and remarked to him that he had just seen Mrs. Washington, and she looked so well that her portrait must again be painted; to which General Washington replied, "that she certainly would sit again, as the temptation of looking well was too strong to be resisted."

Rembrandt recounted in his lecture "Washington and His Portraits" that Gilbert Stuart was painting Washington at the same time: "He could not sit the next day—Mrs. Washington informing me that he was engaged to sit to Mr. Stuart, an Artist from Dublin, who had just come from New York for the purpose." Peale first saw an example of Stuart's finished portrait when he returned to Philadelphia from Charleston in May 1796. He later remembered that it was "Head-size, 25 by 30 inches, with a Crimson Curtain Background–advantageously displayed in a Room of the City hall." He wrote that it was "a beautiful work of Art, tho' not to me a satisfactory likeness." He criticized the florid complexion and, by comparison with Houdon's bust, the inaccurate features, and "the character heavily exaggerated–the eyes too prominent, the nose too flat; the mouth too much distended, & the neck too long; tho' this adds dignity to the head." This description could be of the Vaughan portrait, which another contemporary, Anna Maria Thornton, wife of William Thornton, also criticized. When she saw an example of the Vaughan portrait in 1800, she noted in her diary: "Stewart's original is very like but not an agreeable likeness."

Stuart's success at painting Washington led to two new commissions. One was for the portraits known during Stuart's lifetime as the "Mount Vernon Portraits" [illustrated on pages 40 and 41]. They are now known as the Athenaeum portraits because they were owned by the Boston Athenaeum for more than 150 years. Stuart had requested new sittings because he was dissatisfied with the Vaughan portrait. Washington refused to sit again, until Martha convinced him. She "wished a Portrait for herself; he therefore consented on the express condition that *when finished* it should be hers." Stuart preferred the Mount Vernon portraits to the Vaughan portrait. William Dunlap recorded from John Neagle that

> Mrs. Washington called often to see the general's portrait, and was desirous to possess the painting. . . . One day she called with her husband, and begged to know when she might have it. The general himself never pressed it, but on this occasion, as he and his lady were about to retire, he returned to Mr. Stuart and said he saw plainly of what advantage the picture was to the painter, (who had been constantly employed in copying it, and Stuart had said he could not work so well from another;) he therefore begged the artist to retain the painting at his pleasure.

However, others close to Washington understood that the originals

Martha Washington by Charles Willson Peale, oil on canvas, 72.7 x 59.2 cm (28⅝ x 23⁵/₁₆ in.), 1795. Independence National Historical Park Collection, Philadelphia, Pennsylvania

Martha Washington by James Peale, watercolor on ivory, 4 x 3.2 cm (1⁹/₁₆ x 1¼ in.), 1796. Signed: "I P 1796". The Mount Vernon Ladies' Association, Mount Vernon, Virginia

Right
George Washington (Lansdowne portrait) by Gilbert Stuart, oil on canvas, 243.8 x 152.4 cm (96 x 60 in.), 1796. National Portrait Gallery, Smithsonian Institution, Washington, D.C.; anonymous loan

were intended for Mount Vernon. George Turner, in Philadelphia, wrote his friend William Thornton in Washington on June 2, 1799: "Have the Portraits reached Mount Vernon? I took care, on my arrival, to inform Stuart, in *terms the most cautious*, how gratifying it would be to the General and his lady, to see their *Translation* from Germantown to the Patomak." On January 6, 1800, only three weeks after Washington's death, Thornton complained to English artist William Winstanley about Stuart's treatment of Mrs. Washington.

> I am sorry to be obliged to observe that the late General and his Lady thought themselves extremely ill used by Mr. Stewart, who promised repeatedly the original Painting to them, and always spoke of it as appertaining to them, but never sent it, though frequently solicited. He after took Mrs. Washington's portrait but keeps it unfinished. The Original of the General I think ought to be Mrs. Washington's–and I think Mr. Stewart has not acted honorably in disposing of it. I admire his Genius and Abilities but his inattention to the General's Family certainly was ungrateful after the General sat so repeatedly to serve Mr. Stewart–and to have possessed the Original Picture would have been to Mrs. Washington one of the highest gratifications, now it would be a signal consolation.

Stuart's Athenaeum portrait shows Washington with a very distinct wide-jawed look. According to Rembrandt Peale, Washington was wearing new dentures during the sittings with Stuart, whereas Peale was "fortunate" that his portrait was begun before the new teeth were ready, "and that my Sitter each time came to me with the old Sett furnished him in New York many years before." Stuart commented on this difficulty also: "When I painted him, he had just had a set of false teeth inserted, which accounts for the constrained expression so noticeable about the mouth and lower part of the face." The accuracy of these anecdotes is confirmed by Washington's letter to John Greenwood, his dentist, written on January 20, 1797. Washington returned a set of teeth to Greenwood to be repaired, asking that they be returned "as soon as possible for although I now make use of another sett, they are both uneasy in the mouth and bulge my lips out in such a manner as to make them appear considerably swelled." He asked that "nothing must be done to them which will, in the *least* degree force the lips out than more than *now* do, as it does this too much already."

In 1796 Stuart also painted his first full-length images of Washington, known today as the "Lansdowne" portraits because the first version was the gift of Mrs. William Bingham to William Petty, second Earl of Shelburne and first Marquis of Lansdowne. The marquis, a British supporter of the American cause during the war, was one of the subscribers of Stuart's first portrait of Washington; his name is on the list Stuart drew

up in 1795. Washington agreed to at least one sitting for the full-length, in the spring of 1796. On April 11, Washington wrote the artist:

> Sir: I am under promise to Mrs. Bingham, to set for you to-morrow at nine oclock, and wishing to know if it be convenient to you that I should do so, and whether it shall be at your own house, (as she talked of the State House), I send this note to you, to ask information.

Washington's grandson George Washington Parke Custis later wrote: "It is notorious that it was only by hard begging that Mrs. Bingham obtained the sittings for the marquis of Lansdowne's picture."

The standing portrait depicts Washington as he appeared before Congress in Philadelphia. A young eyewitness who saw Washington speak at the opening of Congress, later remembered,

> Washington was dressed precisely as Stuart has painted him in Lord Landsdowne's full-length portrait—in a full suit of the richest black velvet, with diamond kneebuckles, and square silver buckles set upon shoes japanned with the most scrupulous neatness, black silk stockings, his shirt ruffled at the breast and wrists, a light dress sword, his hair profusely powdered, fully dressed, so as to project at the sides, and gathered behind in a silk bag, ornamented with a large rose of black riband. He held his cocked hat, which had a large black cockade on one side of it, in his hand, as he advanced toward the chair, and, when seated, laid it on the table.

The portrait includes furniture symbolic of the new American republic, as well as books titled *American Revolution,* and *Constitution & Laws of the United States,* and a silver inkstand engraved with the Washington family coat of arms. The portrait, sent to London in the fall of 1796, was described in detail in the London *Oracle and Public Advertiser* on May 15, 1797:

> The figure is above the middle height, well proportioned, and exceedingly graceful. The countenance is mild and yet forcible. The eye, of a light grey, is rendered marking by a brow to which physiognomy attaches the sign of power. The forehead is ample, the nose aquiline, the mouth regular and persuasive. The face is distinguishable for muscle rather than flesh, and this may be said of the whole person. The dress he wears is plain black velvet; he has his sword on, upon the hilt of which one hand rests while the other is extended, as the figure is standing and addressing the Hall of Assembly. . . . The Marquis of Lansdowne is exceedingly flattered by the present.

Another version of the portrait was described in *The Time Piece* at the time of its exhibition in New York City in 1798:

General Washington (large as life) represented in the position of addressing Congress the last time, before his retirement from public life. . . . He is surrounded with allegorical emblems of his public life in the service of his country, which are highly illustrative of the great and tremendous storms which have frequently prevailed. These storms have abated, and the appearance of the rainbow is introduced in the background as a sign.

A Return to Familial Images

By the end of Washington's second term, the couple was eager to return to Mount Vernon. A few additional portraits were made before they left Philadelphia. One was a miniature of Martha, painted by James Peale in 1796 [illustrated on page 44]. It is probably the one described in Martha's letter of January 3, 1796, to her granddaughter Nelly:

> I was in hopes my dear child to have had a picture drawn of me for you before this I have set several times–the picture is not yet done nor do I know when it will be ready to send to you as the painter beged I would not hurry him–and as I know the only value of a picture is the likeness it bears to the person it is taken for–I shall wait till he brings it to me.

She referred again to the portrait in her letter of January 14 when discussing a trunk that she had arranged to send to Nelly's sister, Martha Peter: "I have put into it everything that you have asked for, and every thing I promised you, when I send the Picture which I hope to have ready to send by Mrs. Bassett with two pocket handkerchiefs which will make six."

In addition, two profile portraits were made of the Washingtons in 1796 or 1797, at the time that their two youngest grandchildren and George Washington Motier Lafayette, the son of the Marquis de Lafayette, were also portrayed. The artist, English painter and pastelist James Sharples (1751/1752-1811), came to the United States in the mid-1790s with his wife Ellen Sharples and his three youngest children. Washington paid for Sharples's portraits of George Washington Parke Custis and young Lafayette on May 10, 1796. The portrait of Washington is the last for which he sat; the sittings are undocumented. Sharples drew the outlines of the portraits with a mechanical instrument, which ensured physiognomic accuracy. As Custis later wrote, it was "an admirable likeness, the profile taken by an instrument, and critically correct." The Sharples portrait of Washington at the National Portrait Gallery [illustrated on page 49] is one of about thirty duplicates made by

The Washington Family
by Edward Savage, oil on
canvas, 215.3 x 284.2 cm
(84¾ x 111⅞ in.),
1789–1796. National
Gallery of Art,
Washington, D.C.;
Andrew W. Mellon
Collection, 1940.1.2

the artist and his wife. Framed with it is an inscription by Eliza Parke Custis:

> This is an Original Portrait of Genl Washington taken in 1797–it was painted by Mr. Sharpless & is an exact likeness except the complexion Genl Washington was very fair with light brown almost auburn hair–he had not a black beard. He had artificial teeth but so well fixed, that they did not disfigure his mouth–his hair was thin, craped & dress with powder & pomatum as this profile.

Sharples also drew several portraits of Washington in a three-quarter pose. Some of the portraits were advertised for public sale. Sharples also made two duplicates of the profile of Martha Washington, including one owned by Daniel Wadsworth with a pendant portrait of Washington. He gave the portraits to the Wadsworth Athenaeum in 1847. James B. Hosmer, a trustee of the museum, recorded the gift in his diary and added: "Mr. Wadsworth says the likeness of Washington is capitol-perfect, of Mrs. Washington very good but not equal to the general. They were taken for and at the request of Colonel Wadsworth." Daniel

Wadsworth's father Jeremiah had been commissary general to the Continental army.

The most ambitious of the last portraits was also the only group portrait [illustrated on page 48], painted by Edward Savage, the Massachusetts artist who had painted the Washingtons in 1789-1790. *The Washington Family* depicts George and Martha Washington along with Nelly and George Washington Parke Custis. The African American at the right has been tentatively identified as William Lee, the slave who had served Washington during the Revolution. The setting includes a view of the Potomac River. On the table is a map of the new city of Washington, which appears to be the engraving of Pierre L'Enfant's plan for the new capital, published in 1792. Savage began this large group portrait when he first painted the Washingtons, and worked on it for about six years. The portraits are based on his earlier images, with some changes in position and other details. Savage first exhibited the finished painting in his Columbian Gallery in Philadelphia on February 22, 1796, Washington's sixty-third birthday. When he made an engraving of the portrait in 1798, Washington purchased four framed examples. The painting is a unique image of the first President in his combined civic, military, and familial roles, an important attempt by a contemporary artist to capture and idealize the image of the first President.

The desire to preserve Washington's appearance and make a visual record of his character led to a wide range of images that mainly agree on several features: oval face, bony facial structure, blue eyes, long nose, and thin lips. Beyond this, they often convey differing images of the first President. Early assessments of the portraits of Washington also varied, a reflection as much, perhaps, of their meaning as of their accuracy. Josiah Quincy "always declared that the portrait by Savage in the College dining room in Harvard Hall at Cambridge, was the best likeness he had ever seen of Washington, though its merits as a work of art are but small." The portrait by Wertmüller was admired by an anonymous writer in the *National Intelligencer*, who described it as "the one of all others most resembling him." George Washington Parke Custis, however, questioned whether it was from life, asking "where is the distinguishing feature in the physiognomy of the chief at that period–the projection of the under lip?" John Pintard recorded in his diary about a visit to Mount Vernon on July 31, 1801: "There are several prints, medals, medallions, and miniatures of the President in the house, none of which please Mrs. W. She does not think Stuart's celebrated painting a true resemblance." However, the most memorable comment about portraits of Washington belongs to John Neal, an early-nineteenth-century writer and art critic:

> Stuart says, and there is no fact more certain, that he [Washington] was a
> man of terrible passions; the sockets of his eyes; the breadth of his nose
> and nostrils; the deep broad expression of strength and solemnity upon
> his forehead, were all a proof of this. So, Stuart painted him; and, though
> a better likeness of him were shown to us, we should reject it; for, the only
> idea that we now have of George Washington, is associated with Stuart's
> Washington.

He added, "If Washington should appear on earth, just as he sat to
Stuart, I am sure that he would be treated as an imposter, when compared
with Stuart's likeness of him, unless he produced his credentials."

Notes on Sources

"It is indeed almost as difficult," Fisher Ames, "Eulogy on Washington" (1800), in *Works of Fisher Ames* (Boston, 1809), p. 130, quoted by Elizabeth Bryant Johnston, *Original Portraits of Washington, Including Statues, Monuments, and Medals* (Boston: James R. Osgood, 1882), title page.

Contemporary Descriptions
"The General is about," unidentified visitor, quoted in Francis Rufus Bellamy, *The Private Life of George Washington* (New York: Thomas Y. Crowell, 1951), p. 341. "Let me take a review," *The Diary of William Maclay and Other Notes on Senate Debates*, ed. Kenneth R. Bowling and Helen E. Veit (Baltimore: Johns Hopkins University Press, 1988), pp. 365-66. "The height of his person," Isaac Weld Jr., *Travels through the States of North America and the Provinces of Upper and Lower Canada, during the Years 1795, 1796 and 1797*, 2 vols. (4th ed.; London, 1807), vol. 1, p. 105. "She received me," Abigail Adams to Mary Cranch, June 28, 1789, in Stewart Mitchell, ed., *New Letters of Abigail Adams, 1788–1801* (Boston: Houghton Mifflin, 1947), p. 13. "Mrs. Washington is one," July 12, 1789, in Mitchell, *Abigail Adams*, p. 15. "Mrs. Washington is a most friendly," October 11, 1789, in Mitchell, *Abigail Adams*, p. 30. "Something older than the President," David John Jeremy, ed., *Henry Wansey and His American Journal, 1794* (Philadelphia: American Philosophical Society, 1970), p. 100.

Portrait Miniatures
"In for a penny," Washington to Francis Hopkinson, May 16, 1785, W. W. Abbot and Dorothy Twohig, eds., *The Papers of George Washington: Confederation Series* (Charlottesville: University Press of Virginia, 1992), vol. 2, pp. 561-62. "About twelve oClock," Henrietta Liston to her uncle, December 9, 1796, in Bradford Perkins, "A Diplomat's Wife in Philadelphia: Letters of Henrietta Liston, 1796-1800," *William and Mary Quarterly* 3d ser., 11 (October 1954): 606. "The portrait I first Sketched," Savage to Washington, October 6, 1793, quoted in Louisa Dresser, "Edward Savage, 1761-1817," *Art in America* 40 (autumn 1952): 198. "Sat for Mr. Rammage," Donald Jackson and Dorothy Twohig, eds., *The Diaries of George Washington*, 6 vols. (Charlottesville: University Press of Virginia, 1976-1979), vol. 5, p. 451. "Sat about two Oclock," Jackson and Twohig, *Washington Diaries*, vol. 5, p. 451. "Accept, with goodness," Moustier to Washington, May 11, 1790, in Dorothy Twohig et al., eds., *The Papers of George Washington: Presidential Series*, 8 vols. to date (Charlottesville: University Press of Virginia, 1987-1999), vol. 5, p. 392. "In presenting the enclosed," Washington to Anne Willing Bingham, March 16, 1791 (or 1796), Mount Vernon Ladies' Association of the Union; see *Annual Report: The Mount Vernon Ladies' Association of the Union, 1968* (Mount Vernon, Va., 1969), pp. 20-25, 33.

State Portraits
"In behalf of the *Ladies,*" selectmen of Boston to Washington, October 27, 1789, George Washington Papers, Manuscript Division, Library of Congress, partially quoted in Twohig et al., *Washington Papers: Presidential Series*, vol. 4, p. 237. "That I would have it drawn," *Washington Diaries*, vol. 5, p. 478. "Gullager, the painter," Dr. Jeremy Belknap, Almanac, entry of October 27, 1789, Massachusetts Historical Society, quoted in Marvin Sadik, *Christian Gullager: Portrait Painter to Federal America* (Washington, D.C.: National Portrait Gallery, 1976), p. 74. "Sat two hours," *Washington Diaries*, vol. 5, p. 490. Major William Jackson served as Washington's private secretary; Mr. Brick is believed to be Samuel Breck, whose Boston sailcloth factory Washington visited on October 28. "At

the time the likeness," Charles Gulager to Henry Gulager, March 5, 1832, quoted in Louisa Dresser, "Christian Gullager: An Introduction to His Life and Some Representative Examples of His Work," *Art in America* 37 (July 1949): 111. "When you were in," Willard to Washington, November 7, 1789, *Washington Papers: Presidential Series,* vol. 4, p. 280. "From a wish that I have," Washington to Willard, December 23, 1789, *Washington Papers: Presidential Series,* vol. 4, p. 432. "To commemorate his arrival," in "Resolution of the City Council of Charleston," May 7, 1791, in Anna Wells Rutledge, *Catalogue of Paintings and Sculpture in the Council Chamber, City Hall, Charleston, South Carolina* (Charleston, S.C.: City Council of Charleston, 1943), p. 30. "To give his military character," Theodore Sizer, ed., *The Autobiography of Colonel John Trumbull, Patriot-Artist, 1756–1843* (New Haven: Yale University Press, 1953), pp. 170–71. "Oppressed as the President was," Sizer, *Trumbull,* p. 171. "To inform you," Lear to Pintard, August 24, 1790, *Washington Papers: Presidential Series,* vol. 6, p. 323. Letterbook, vol. 22, Washington Papers, Library of Congress, partially quoted in John C. Fitzpatrick, ed., *The Writings of George Washington from the Original Manuscript Sources, 1745–1799,* 39 vols. (1931–1944; reprint, Westport, Conn.: Greenwood Press, 1970), vol. 31, p. 96n. "Pd. Mr. Peale," Stephen Decatur Jr., *Private Affairs of George Washington; From the Records and Accounts of Tobias Lear, Esquire, His Secretary* (Boston: Houghton Mifflin, 1933), p. 240.

European Artists and American Admirers

"A Monument Designed," Ceracchi to Washington, October 31, 1791, enclosing a description of the monument, quoted in Ulysse Desportes, "Giuseppe Ceracchi in America and His Busts of George Washington," *Art Quarterly* 26, no. 2 (summer 1963): 147. "With the reluctance," Washington to Ceracchi, March 9, 1795, in Fitzpatrick, *Writings of Washington,* vol. 34, p. 137. Although the draft is in Washington's handwriting, the final letter was signed by Bartholomew Dandridge, Washington's secretary. "Besides the generality," original letter and duplicate, Washington Papers, Library of Congress, quoted in Desportes, "Ceracchi in America," p. 150, who misread "solidity" as "wisdom," and in Joseph E. Fields, comp., *"Worthy Partner": The Papers of Martha Washington* (Westport, Conn.: Greenwood Press, 1994), p. 239, where the word is not deciphered. "Finds herself at a loss," Fields, *"Worthy Partner,"* p. 263. "The modern American Wallace," Earl of Buchan, quoted without identification in Martha J. Lamb, "Unpublished Washington Portraits: Some of the Early Artists," *Magazine of American History* 19, no. 4 (April 1888): 278. "An honest artist," Earl of Buchan to Washington, June 28, 1791, *Washington Papers: Presidential Series,* vol. 8, p. 306. "The excitation in the mind," Robertson, manuscript account (unlocated), quoted in Lamb, "Unpublished Washington Portraits," p. 276, and in Edith Robertson Cleveland, "Archibald Robertson and His Portraits of the Washingtons," *Century Magazine* 40 (May 1890): 7. "Very readily condescended," Archibald Robertson to the Earl of Buchan, October 20, 1792, Library, Mount Vernon Ladies' Association of the Union. "In his family," Robertson, manuscript account, quoted in Cleveland, "Robertson," p. 10. "Collection of portraits," Robertson, manuscript account, quoted in Lamb, "Unpublished Washington Portraits," p. 276, and Cleveland, "Robertson," p. 7. "In evidence of," Trumbull to Elizabeth Parke Custis, May 1, 1829, quoted in Helen Cooper, *John Trumbull: The Hand and Spirit of a Painter* (New Haven: Yale University Art Gallery, 1982), p. 118. "Gave Mr. Trumbull's servant," in "Washington's Household Account Book, 1793–1797," *Pennsylvania Magazine of History and Biography* 29 (1905): 404. "For 2 picture frames," "Washington's Household Account Book, 1793–1797," *PMHB* 30 (1906): 44. "Promised to present," Henry Lee to Washington, June 20, 1792, in William Moseley Brown, *George Washington, Freemason* (Richmond: Garrett & Massie, Inc., 1952), p. 102. "A professional man," Fitzpatrick, *Writings of Washington,* vol. 32, pp. 83–84. "He will, however, sit," Williams to Lee, July 3, 1792, in Brown, *Washington,* p. 103. "But although history," Elisha Cullen Dick, James Taylor, and Charles Simms to Washington, August 29, 1793, in Washington Papers, Library of Congress. "Williams Pinxit," portrait file, Catalog of American Portraits, National Portrait Gallery, from the research notes of John Hill Morgan recorded on the photograph mount for this portrait, Frick Art Reference Library, New York. "Of the painting," George Washington Parke Custis, *Recollections and Private Memoirs of Washington* (Washington, D.C.: W. H. Moore, 1859), p. 526. "Ambitious of drawing himself," Rembrandt Peale, "Reminiscences: Adolph Ulric Wertmüller," *The Crayon* 11, no. 14 (October 3, 1855), in Michel Benisovich, "The Sale of the Studio of Adolph-Ulrich Wertmüller," *Art Quarterly* 16, no. 1 (spring 1953): 37. "The good fortune to," Sundvall to Wertmüller, October 20, 1795, quoted in translation in Franklin D. Scott, *Wertmüller: Artist and Immigrant Farmer* (Chicago: Swedish Pioneer Historical Society, 1963), p. 8. "Complied on the same principle," Washington to Ceracchi, March 9, 1795, in Fitzpatrick, *Writings of Washington*, vol. 34, p. 138. "For the Original," invoice with Ceracchi's letter of May 7, 1795, to Washington, in Washington Papers, Library of Congress; the accompanying letter is quoted in Desportes, "Ceracchi in America," p. 166. "The abilities of our infant republic," Washington to Ceracchi, March 9, 1795, in Fitzpatrick, *Writings of Washington*, vol. 34, p. 139.

Family Portraits
"The wish nearest," paraphrase by William Armstrong of a letter from Washington to Martha Custis Peter, now unlocated, "Some New Washington Relics. I: From the Collection of Mrs. B. W. Kennon," *Century Illustrated Monthly Magazine* 40 (May 1890): 14. "*No other wish,*" quoted in Edmund Law Rogers, "Some New Washington Relics. II: From the Collection of Edmund Law Rogers, Esq.," *Century Illustrated Monthly Magazine* 40 (May 1890): 23. "Went to Philadelphia," William Dunlap, *History of the Rise and Progress of the Arts of Design in the United States,* 2 vols. (New York, 1834), vol. 1, p. 430. "Pd Wm Robertson," "Washington's Household Account Book, 1793-1797," *PMHB* 30 (1906): 326. "Was altogether a failure," Dunlap, *History*, vol. 1, p. 430. "One remarkable deviation," Dunlap, *History*, vol. 1, p. 430. "Miniature of the President," Field to Gilmore, Dreer Collection, Historical Society of Pennsylvania, quoted in Harry Piers, *Robert Field: Portrait Painter in Oils, Miniature and Water-Colours and Engraver* (New York: Frederic Fairchild Sherman, 1927), pp. 10-11. "A Portrait of Alexander Hamilton," *American Minerva; an Evening Advertiser,* May 25, 1795, quoted in Rita Susswein Gottesman, *The Arts and Crafts in New York, 1777-1799: Advertisements and News Items from New York City Newspapers* (New York: New-York Historical Society, 1954), p. 38. "Four Plates," *Maryland Journal,* April 20, 1795, partially quoted in Alfred Coxe Prime, *The Arts and Crafts in Philadelphia, Maryland and South Carolina,* vol. 2 (1933; reprint, New York: Da Capo Press, 1969), p. 68, and in Piers, *Robert Field,* p. 13.

Portraits by Gilbert Stuart and the Peales
"I expect to make," John Dowling Herbert, *Irish Varieties for the Last Fifty Years* (London, 1836), quoted in William T. Whitley, *Gilbert Stuart* (1932; reprint, New York: Da Capo Press, 1969), p. 85. "Toward the spring," Jane Stuart, "The Stuart Portraits of Washington," *Scribner's Monthly* 12, no. 3 (July 1876): 369. "A list of gentlemen," Stuart, "Portraits of Washington," p. 373; John Hill Morgan and Mantle Fielding, *The Life Portraits of Washington and their Replicas* (Philadelphia: published for the subscribers, 1931), p. 227. "When not too angular," Johann Caspar Lavater, *Essays on Physiognomy, Designed to Promote the Knowledge and Love of Mankind,* trans. Henry Hunter, 3 vols. (London, 1789-1798), vol. 3, pp. 435, 436. "Some colored coat," William Sullivan, *Familiar Letters on Public Characters and Public Events from the Peace of 1783, to the Peace of 1815* (Boston, 1834), p. 90. "It was in the Autumn," Rembrandt Peale, "Washington and His Portraits," manuscript, 1858, in Gustavus A. Eisen, *Portraits of Washington,* 3 vols. (New York: Robert Hamilton and Associates, 1932), vol. 1, appendix, p. 308. "That General Washington," Dunlap, *History,* vol. 1, p. 206. "His father, Charles Willson Peale," catalogue of the sale of Peale's museum in 1854, quoted in Charles Coleman Sellers, *Por-

traits and Miniatures by Charles Willson Peale (Philadelphia: American Philosophical Society, 1952), p. 243, no. 957. "He could not sit," Peale, "Washington and His Portraits," in Eisen, *Portraits of Washington,* vol. 1, p. 308. "Head-size, 25 by 30 inches," Peale, "Washington and His Portraits," in Eisen, *Portraits of Washington,* vol. 1, p. 311. "Stewart's original," diary of Anna Maria Brodeau Thornton, entry dated July 5, 1800, William Thornton Papers, Manuscript Division, Library of Congress. "Mount Vernon Portraits," Stuart's advertisement announcing plans to publish an engraving of the "Mount Vernon Portrait" appeared in the *Philadelphia Aurora,* June 12, 1800, in Prime, *The Arts and Crafts in Philadelphia, Maryland and South Carolina,* p. 34. "Wished a Portrait for herself," Peale, "Washington and His Portraits," in Eisen, *Portraits of Washington,* vol. 1, p. 311. "Mrs. Washington called often," Dunlap, *History,* vol. 1, p. 198. "Have the Portraits," George Turner to William Thornton, Thornton Papers, Library of Congress; transcript courtesy of Margaret Christman, National Portrait Gallery. "I am sorry to be obliged," Thornton to William Winstanley, January 6, 1800, Thornton Papers, Library of Congress, transcript courtesy of Margaret Christman. "Fortunate . . . that my Sitter," Peale, "Washington and His Portraits," in Eisen, *Portraits of Washington,* vol. 1, p. 309. "When I painted him," Stuart, "Portraits of Washington," p. 370. "As soon as possible," Washington to John Greenwood, January 20, 1797, in Fitzpatrick, *Writings of Washington,* vol. 35, pp. 370-71. "Sir: I am under promise," Washington to Gilbert Stuart, reproduced in Eisen, *Portraits of Washington,* vol. 1, p. 59, pl. 5, and quoted in Morgan and Fielding, *Life Portraits of Washington,* pp. 358-59. "It is notorious," Custis, *Recollections of Washington,* p. 526. "Washington was dressed," Sigma [pseudonym], "The Character and Personal Appearance of Washington," *National Intelligencer,* February 1847, quoted in Custis, *Recollections of Washington,* p. 491. "The figure is above," quoted in Whitley, *Stuart,* pp. 99-100. "General Washington (large as life)," Gardner Baker, advertisement dated February 5, 1798, quoted in Morgan and Fielding, *Life Portraits of Washington,* p. 360.

A Return to Familial Images

"I was in hopes," Martha Washington to Eleanor Parke Custis, January 3, 1796, Fields, *"Worthy Partner,"* p. 289. "I have put into it," Martha Washington to Eleanor Parke Custis, January 14, 1796, Fields, *"Worthy Partner,"* p. 290. "An admirable likeness," Custis, *Recollections of Washington,* p. 518. "This is an Original": The inscription, attached to the frame of the portrait, is reproduced in Katharine McCook Knox, *The Sharples; Their Portraits of George Washington and His Contemporaries; A Diary and an Account of the Life and Work of James Sharples and His Family in England and America* (1930; reprint, New York: Da Capo Press, 1972), p. 76, fig. 42. "Mr. Wadsworth says," quoted in Richard Saunders with Helen Raye, *Daniel Wadsworth, Patron of the Arts* (Hartford: Wadsworth Atheneum, 1981), p. 59. "Always declared that," quoted in Dresser, "Savage," p. 193, from Edmund Quincy, *Life of Josiah Quincy of Massachusetts* (Boston: Tichnor and Fields, 1867), p. 51. "The one of all," quoted by Johnston, *Original Portraits of Washington,* p. 53, and Eisen, *Portraits of Washington,* vol. 1, p. 895, without specific citation. "Where is the distinguishing feature," Custis, *Recollections of Washington,* p. 526. "There are several prints," quoted in Armstrong, "Some New Washington Relics," p. 16. "Stuart says," John Neal, *Randolph, a Novel* (1823) in Harold Edward Dickson, ed., *Observations on American Art; Selections from the Writings of John Neal (1793–1876)* (State College, Penn.: Pennsylvania State College, 1943), pp. 2-3.

For Further Reading ∼

Flexner, James Thomas. *George Washington and the New Nation (1783–1793)*. Boston and Toronto: Little, Brown, 1970.

———. *George Washington, Anguish and Farewell (1793–1799)*. Boston and Toronto: Little, Brown, 1972.

Floyd, William Barrow. "The Portraits and Paintings at Mount Vernon from 1754 to 1799." *Antiques Magazine* 100 (December 1971): 894-99.

Giuseppe Ceracchi, Scultore Giacobino (1751–1801). Rome: Palazzo dei Conservatori, 1989.

Kaminski, John P., and Jill Adair McCaughan, eds. *A Great and Good Man: George Washington in the Eyes of His Contemporaries*. Madison, Wis.: Madison House, 1989.

McLanathan, Richard. *Gilbert Stuart*. New York: Harry N. Abrams, 1986.

Miller, Lillian B., ed. *The Peale Family: Creation of a Legacy (1770–1870)*. New York: Abbeville Press, 1996.

Morgan, Edmund S. *The Genius of George Washington*. New York: W. W. Norton, 1981.

Sadik, Marvin. *Christian Gullager, Portrait Painter to Federal America*. Washington, D.C.: National Portrait Gallery, 1976.

Smith, Richard Norton. *Patriarch: George Washington and the New American Nation*. Boston and New York: Houghton Mifflin, 1993.

Stewart, Robert G. "Portraits of George and Martha Washington." *Antiques Magazine* 135 (February 1989): 474-79.

Wick, Wendy C. *George Washington, an American Icon: The Eighteenth-Century Graphic Portraits*. Washington, D.C.: National Portrait Gallery, 1982.

Wills, Garry. *Cincinnatus: George Washington and the Enlightenment*. Garden City, N.Y.: Doubleday, 1984.